Original title:
Petal Trails

Copyright © 2025 Creative Arts Management OÜ
All rights reserved.

Author: Olivia Sterling
ISBN HARDBACK: 978-1-80566-746-9
ISBN PAPERBACK: 978-1-80566-816-9

Whirling Among the Garden's Eyelids

In the garden where the daisies dance,
Worms wear tuxedos, what a chance!
Butterflies giggle, floating high,
While bumblebees buzz and wave goodbye.

The roses gossip, oh so sweet,
About the fancy shoes on a tiny beet.
Sunflowers peep through their big, round hats,
Claiming they're the best at dodging chats.

Twirling tulips try their best to spin,
A dandelion's laughter makes them grin.
The ladybugs stomp in a conga line,
While ants argue over who gets to dine.

Sneaky snails race, but move quite slow,
Mighty oak trees wave with a gentle flow.
Grasshoppers leap with a hop and a skip,
While the daisies dream of a road trip!

Through the muddy puddles, the critters play,
Creating splash zones—it's a wild day!
And as the sun sets, all take a bow,
In the garden's charm, we find joy now.

Footprints on the Garden Path

Bumbling bees buzz round the blooms,
While ladybugs dance on vast green looms.
A snail claims victory, oh what a race,
Leaving a trail, a sticky embrace.

A rabbit hops in, with style and grace,
Chasing his shadow all over the place.
The daisies giggle as squirrels spin,
Each prancing prank leaves us all in a grin.

Mosaic of Nature's Secrets

Sunlight winks through leaves of jade,
As frogs croak jokes from their leafy spade.
A butterfly flutters, its wings all a-gleam,
Stealing the show like it's living a dream.

Caterpillars munch with a squishy delight,
Planning a party that starts in the night.
While crickets serenade with tunes so spry,
Filling the air as the stars say hi.

Scented Dreams in the Wind

Whiffs of lavender play hide and seek,
In a colorful realm where flowers peak.
A dandelion wishes it could be tall,
Instead, it chuckles as seeds start to sprawl.

The wind tells tales that twist and twirl,
Of bees that lost their lunch in a whirl.
As the sun sets low in a radiant blaze,
Nature erupts with a giggly craze.

A Tapestry of Colorful Steps

Footed by mismatched socks in a line,
The garden's a stage, and oh, it's divine!
A toddler stumbles, then wobbles away,
Discovering colors in a humorous way.

A parade of ants marches with flair,
Always in sync; they form quite a pair.
As clouds float by on a fluffy delight,
Nature's jesters hold court every night.

Lost in a Garden's Embrace

In a garden of blooms, I took a wrong turn,
Tripped on a tulip, watched as it burned.
A bee stole my sandwich, oh what a plight,
I waved him away, but he put up a fight.

With roses a-dancing, the lilies all sway,
I laughed at the chaos, come what may.
The daisies all chuckled, they knew my fate,
I'd lost my way, but I found my mate.

Nature's Canvas Unfurled

The daisies were giggling, quite carefree,
While I tried to paint, oh dear me!
I dipped my brush in a pot full of green,
But ended up splattering, oh what a scene!

With petals a-pouting, in colors so bright,
They whispered, 'Stay calm, just hold on tight.'
So I painted my shoes, then took a quick trip,
Now the garden's my canvas, I'm part of the script.

The Soothing Whisper of Floral Waves

The flowers were chatting, it's hard to believe,
They mentioned my socks, which I need to retrieve.
In lilac and blue, the chitchat was grand,
But all I could hear was a butterfly band.

They danced like confetti, both funny and wild,
I laughed with the petals, like a happy child.
As blooms shared their secrets on summers so hot,
I realized my life's just a colorful spot.

A Journey Marked by Scent

I wandered through scents, a bizarre kind of maze,
Rosemary there, made me feel quite dazed.
With lavender laughs and a whiff of surprise,
I sneezed like a monster, oh the garden's demise!

The violets chuckled, the marigolds swayed,
Pointing at me, oh, what a charade!
Yet in every bloom, was a giggle in sight,
So I joined in the laughter, it felt just right.

Flutters of Color on the Breeze

A butterfly wore polka dots,
Danced with a bee in silly knots.
They twirled through the garden, oh what a sight,
Chasing each other from morning till night.

The flowers giggled, waving their heads,
While ants marched on, ignoring their threads.
A ladybug chuckled, sipping her tea,
Saying, "Who knew chaos could feel so free!"

The Allure of Wandering Blooms

A daisy dreamed of a grand parade,
With roses in tiaras, all beautifully displayed.
But when they stepped out in their finest attire,
They tripped over roots; oh, what a quagmire!

Sunflowers swayed, pointing to the sky,
While violets whispered, "Don't ask me why!"
They waved to the breeze as they turned in the sun,
As laughter and petals tangled in fun.

Secrets Beneath the Canopy

Beneath the leaves, the gossip flowed,
Mushrooms in circles with stories bestowed.
Fungi debated on the best kind of light,
While pinecones rolled by, just getting in sight.

The squirrels joined in with acorn debates,
Arguing fiercely for their tasty plates.
But when the wind howled, they all took a clue,
And laughed as they scattered, dancing anew.

Interludes of Wildflower Grace

In a wild place where flowers play tricks,
They sported their colors, had parties with ticks.
With petals adorned in the wildest designs,
They danced under stars, sipping nectar at shrines.

A curious fox joined the fun with a grin,
Said, "A dance with the daisies? Where do I begin?"
The night filled with giggles and rustling leaves,
As nature concocted its playful reprieves.

Glimpses into Floral Fantasies

In a garden dressed in hues,
A bee tried on some floral shoes.
He tripped on daisies, oh what a sight,
Dancing clumsily, morning to night.

The tulips giggled, quite amused,
As the squirrel shared his nutty ruse.
He painted petals with his snacks,
Creating colors that earned him flaks.

Butterflies were having tea,
Chatting with a buzzing bumblebee.
They offered him a crumbly scone,
But he flew off, claiming he wasn't alone.

With fairy dust in every swirl,
The flowers made their petals twirl.
In laughter, they found their delight,
Under the moon, a whimsical night.

Unearthing Hidden Blossoms

In the soil, a secret stirs,
A daffodil sings with little slurs.
He whispers tales of garden gnomes,
Telling stories of their hidden homes.

A rose with thorns, oh how he brags,
Wearing a crown made of old rags.
He claimed to be the king of blooms,
But often tripped on birthday plumes.

The orchids winked and took a glance,
At the squirrel's unimpressive dance.
With every hop, he made a fuss,
Bursting laughter, they couldn't trust.

As worms provided comedic bits,
The daisies rolled and cracked some wits.
In this patch of blooming cheer,
Laughter echoed, spreading near.

The Essence of Wind-Kissed Blooms

A breeze came whispering through the greens,
Tickling petals with playful scenes.
The daisy yelled, 'Hey, watch your hair!'
While sunflowers swooned without a care.

Dandelions tossed their seeds in jest,
Each landing in a place, like a test.
They giggled at the things they'd find,
As they floated off, free and blind.

The lilacs burst with fragrant jokes,
Promising to prank the nearby folks.
They sent a blast of sweet perfume,
Making everyone giggle in the gloom.

The ferns all danced, in patterns tight,
Making shapes, oh what a sight!
In this garden, fun never ends,
Where flowers play and humor blends.

Wandering Through Floral Archways

Through an arch of vibrant flair,
A butterfly fancied fancy wear.
He tried on petals, one by one,
Strutting proudly, thinking he was fun.

Petunias blushed, they couldn't hide,
As bees buzzed in, full of pride.
They formed a troupe, an insect show,
Putting on acts, with flower glow.

Lilies rolled their eyes, quite in shock,
As a gnome practiced his tick-tock.
He slipped on blooms, made a racket,
And the roses laughed, clutching their packet.

With every twist in flowery lanes,
The laughter echoed, breaking chains.
In blooms so bright, spirits soared,
A world of humor, forever adored.

Faded Hues in the Meadow

In the grass, I sit and stare,
A dandelion lost its flair.
It sneezed and sent its fluff so high,
To tickle Shakespeare in the sky.

A bee with shades, so chic and cute,
Dances 'round in a fancy suit.
It cracks a joke, then takes a sip,
Of nectar straight from nature's lip.

A snail on a skateboard zooms right past,
Claiming speed records—what a blast!
While daisies giggle, whispering tales,
Of ants doing flips in snuggly mail.

The sun slips down with a rosy grin,
As frogs in tuxes start to spin.
They croak a tune of rhythmic cheer,
In this meadow, joy is clear!

Secrets of the Flowered Walk

Once upon a lilac lane,
A squirrel juggled, oh what pain!
He dropped three acorns, missed his catch,
And landed straight in a nearby patch.

Roses whispered to the breeze,
About how bees can sometimes sneeze.
While daisies dared to wear a crown,
And mused on life's upside-down frown.

A tulip tried to do a dance,
It tripped on grass, but took a chance.
With laughter soft, it found its beat,
And twirled around with happy feet.

At dusk, the flowers share a chat,
Planning parties with a chatty cat.
With petals folded, they all agree,
This secret walk is pure comedy.

The Garden's Silken Path

Upon the path where lilies lie,
A caterpillar waved goodbye.
He took a leap with grand intent,
But ended up in a daisy's tent.

A rose declared, "You're fashion bold!"
While sunflowers glared with petals gold.
They hatched a plan, all in good fun,
To rival clouds — the sky's big gun!

A hedgehog donned a tiny hat,
He strolled on by, saying, "How about that?"
His quills in bloom drew ancient glee,
As bunnies giggled behind the tree.

With moonlit laughter and starlit chat,
They danced along, even a gnat.
In this garden of joy and glee,
Silken paths lead to pure harmony.

Symphony of Blooming Steps

In the woods, the violets sway,
Balloons on vines, they laugh and play.
A rabbit with a bandaged ear,
Dreams of rockstars every year.

The petals hum a merry tune,
While crickets play a jazzy rune.
A ladybug is DJ there,
Spinning records with flair to spare.

The grinning sapling leans to cheer,
As flowers prance, full of good cheer.
And when the night begins to fall,
They waltz and twirl, a sprightly ball.

In a symphony of roots and blooms,
They shake away their worldly glooms.
Nature's party, come one, come all,
Where laughter and fun forever call!

Meandering Among Nature's Treasures

In the garden, I took a stroll,
Tripped on a gnome—what a roll!
He winked at me, his hat askew,
I swear he laughed, how 'bout you?

Bumblebees buzz in a dance,
Chasing flowers, what a chance!
They seem to think they own the place,
While I just try to keep my pace.

Frogs break out in a croaky song,
Singing vibes all day long.
I joined in, but got a stare,
From flowers really unaware!

Lost a shoe in a muddy patch,
Now I'm stuck in this goofy catch.
Nature's treasures, a secret spree,
Will I make it home with just one tree?

The Whispering Wind Through the Blossoms

The breeze whispers to the daffodils,
With secrets only nature fills.
They nod their heads and giggle too,
I wonder what they mean to do!

Caught a nap on a patch of grass,
Dreamed of bugs that danced with sass.
But that critter, oh what a tease,
Kissed my nose then fled with ease!

Fluffy clouds float like cotton candy,
I reach for one; they seem so dandy!
But they just laugh, float a bit high,
"Catch us if you can!" they cry.

Tickled by the grass's green hand,
I roll and tumble—oh, what a land!
With each puff, the giggles swell,
Nature's secret, who can tell?

Unfolding Secrets in Bloom

In a bouquet of colorful sights,
Flowers gossip, oh what delights!
They trade tales of bugs and sun,
And how they think they've finally won.

A lazy snail slides on the scene,
Moving slow, like it's all a dream.
His shell's a home, but waits too long,
Hurry up, buddy, thing's going wrong!

Petunias wear a frowny face,
While daisies have a cheerful grace.
"Why so sad?" I ask the blooms,
"Perhaps a dance?"—they soon consume!

Finally, they all sway in fun,
Beneath the rays of the bright sun.
Nature's humor is truly gold,
In these tales, we all unfold.

Where Sunlight Paints the Ground

Sunlight spills like a painter's brush,
Colors dance with a joyful hush.
The daisies pose in perfect lines,
As ants march by, with secret signs.

A squirrel darts, with nuts in tow,
He's a thief, putting on a show.
Chasing shadows, what a delight,
"Catch me if you can!" he'll invite.

A ladybug dressed in dots of red,
Joined the fun, where all fears fled.
With tiny wings, she starts to twirl,
Nature's charm begins to swirl!

Beneath the trees, a carnival blooms,
Where laughter echoes, and joy resumes.
I grin wide, what a perfect day,
In this funny world, I will play!

Whispers of Blossom Paths

In the garden where daisies chatter,
Bumblebees argue, 'Who's the fatter?'
Tulips giggle, swaying with grace,
While worms steal snacks, what a weird place!

Sunflowers nod to the clouds above,
Sending secrets on rays of love.
Petunias prance with comical flair,
As beetles do a dance without a care!

Gardens hold tales, strange yet sweet,
Where squirrels hold acorns, all can repeat.
Can you hear that? The roses just laughed,
At a snail who slipped, on leaves he grafted!

In silliness blooms, joy finds its way,
Nature's antics brighten each day.
Join the fun, let your worries go,
In the land where wildflowers grow!

Footprints in Fragrant Fields

In fields of orange, yellow, and blue,
A rabbit hops on the path anew.
With each little leap, a flower sighs,
As daisies giggle under sunny skies.

A timid fox sneezes, then he twirls,
Chasing butterflies with little whirls.
Buttercups blush at the antics near,
While crickets play tunes for all to hear!

The daisies debate which makes the best hat,
While sunbeams chase a lazy cat.
Worms wear shades, they soak up the sun,
In these fragrant fields, we all have fun!

So skip through the blooms, let laughter ring,
Every step a new song to sing.
Join the ruckus, don't be shy—
In the fields where giggles seem to fly!

Dance of the Floral Breeze

The roses waltz with tulips in the air,
Their petals swirling without a care.
A dandelion spins like a ballerina,
Admiring the moves, oh what a scene-a!

In this floral fiesta, the thrush takes flight,
Teasing the moths in the soft moonlight.
Lavenders whisper the silliest tunes,
While fireflies glow like dancing balloons.

Daffodils chuckle, oh what a sight,
As they twirl and leap in pure delight.
Their little leaves clap, a delightful sound,
In a dance where joy is always found!

The night hums with laughter, sweet and pure,
As nature's comedy stays demure.
Join in the dance, let your spirit soar,
In the floral breeze, there's always more!

Gentle Prints on Earth

Little paws scamper, leave prints so neat,
Around them, petals create a treat.
With each funny hop and every slight slip,
A playful adventure, an amusing trip!

Bees wear tiny goggles, buzzing away,
While ants march in line, they're starting to play.
In gardens where every clue smells sweet,
Even the grass seems to dance on its feet!

Frogs leap in puddles, they cause such a splash,
While butterflies twirl, their colors a bash.
A squirrel in mischief, steals all the seeds,
In this playful world, nature's the lead!

Together they weave a tapestry bright,
Where laughter and joy take joyful flight.
So step on the earth, leave your own cheer,
In this moment of fun, there's nothing to fear!

Enchanted Steps in the Meadow

In the meadow, I take a hop,
Chasing butterflies, I just can't stop.
A squirrel giggles, causing me to trip,
I land on soft grass, with a silly flip.

Daisies dance in the warm sun's glow,
But watch out for bees, they steal the show.
With a flower crown atop my head,
I declare myself queen, a flowerbed fed!

A rabbit appears, thinks he can race,
I challenge him, oh, what a silly face!
We leap 'round puddles, splashing with glee,
Nature's playground, just wild and free!

The day ends with laughter, stories galore,
Under starlit skies, we want more!
With friends so dear, the meadow's our throne,
Who knew grass could seem so much fun on its own?

Wandering Where Flowers Bloom

I wander through fields, oh what a sight,
Flowers in colors, a pure delight!
With each step I take, a petal will sway,
I might just embarrass myself today!

A busy bee buzzes, calls me a fool,
He's got more nectar, I'm just here to drool.
Rose bushes snicker as I walk by,
"Keep it quiet, they'll hear," I sigh!

In a daisy patch, I find a bright hat,
A little too big, but that's where it's at.
I strut like a model, with flower flair,
Who needs a runway when you've got fresh air?

Oh, the joy of blooms and their silly dance,
Inviting me in for a joyous prance.
I'll twirl and I'll laugh till the sun bids adieu,
In this vibrant world, there's always room for two!

The Resonance of Sweet Scents

The air is a symphony of floral delight,
I sniff a sunflower, what a strange sight!
A whiff of the lilac, my nose takes a twist,
Now it's scratching and sneezing, oh what a tryst!

Pollen parade, what a fussy affair,
The roses protest, "Please don't come near!"
"I'm just here to sniff, not to shake your petals,"
As they huff and they puff, my scent rebels.

Lavender whispers, "Come take a rest,"
I plop down for tea, feeling so blessed.
But bees think my snack is quite the buffet,
"Not on my lap!" I yell, what else can I say?

With scents swirling wildly, it fills me with joy,
These floral fragrances—nature's ploy!
A giggle erupts from the daisies nearby,
"We'll bloom all around you, oh my, oh my!"

The Harmony of Green and Bloom

In the garden, all's bright, a joyous scene,
Where green meets the bright, like ketchup on beans!
I trip on a root, falling with flair,
The tulips applaud, "You've got style, we swear!"

With grass like a carpet, I'll roll and I'll cheer,
Mixing laughter with petals, what a good idea!
I pop up like daisies, all silly and spry,
Waving to robins that fly slice of pie!

Giggling with smirks at my muddy old shoe,
Who knew such fun could be found in the dew?
A dandelion shouts, "Make a wish, friend!"
I blow it away, where mischief won't end.

As the sun sets low, the laughter still thrives,
Nature's silly antics fill up our lives.
With every bloom, and kerfuffle so sweet,
Life is the garden where giggles repeat!

Echoes Beneath the Blossoms

Under the trees, I slip and slide,
Chasing bees with newfound pride.
They buzz around like they own the place,
While I trip over roots, what a hilarious chase!

The flowers giggle, bright as can be,
As I tumble down, ungracefully.
With petals in hair, I wear a crown,
In this floral chaos, I never frown!

A squirrel laughs from the high branch,
I can't climb up; oh, what a chance!
Leaves turn to confetti, it's quite the scene,
Nature's own circus, if you know what I mean!

So here I dance, legs going wild,
Among the blooms, forever a child.
Life's silly moments, I seize with glee,
Beneath these blossoms, forever carefree!

Dance of the Fallen Leaves

Leaves are falling, I start to twirl,
One sticks to my nose, oh what a swirl!
With every gust, it's a leafy fight,
As they dance around, oh what a sight!

I slip on a leaf, land flat on my back,
Those sneaky leaves sure know how to attack!
The trees are laughing, I hear their glee,
Can't trust the ground; it's plotting against me!

A windstorm howls, they take to the sky,
I'm left here flailing, oh my, oh my!
With arms outstretched like a drunken bird,
Between leaf piles, I've utterly blurred!

Yet amidst the laughter, I rise with a grin,
For every slip leads to joy from within.
In this silly dance, life spins around,
With fallen leaves, fun can always be found!

The Journey of Delicate Blades

Grass blades whisper, swaying on cue,
They giggle and wiggle, as if they all knew.
Tickle my toes, the grass makes me laugh,
One silly blade thinks it's a giraff!

Trying to run, I stumble and fumble,
Trapped in a patch, it's a grassy tumble.
The blades cheer me on, a botanical crew,
"Don't worry," they say, "we'll grow back anew!"

A dandelion mocks with its fluffy plume,
"Think you can catch me? You'll meet your doom!"
With every step, I trip and I glide,
In this grassy wonder, I can't help but ride!

So hand me the sun and a smile so wide,
With each whimsy plunge, I'm filled with pride.
A journey in green, so quirky and light,
Among delicate blades, life's a hilarious flight!

Embracing the Floral Breeze

In the floral fields where the breezes play,
I chase after blooms that float away.
They twirl and they spin, in a colorful race,
As I trip on my shoelace, what a funny place!

A butterfly lands right on my nose,
Startled, I sneeze, and off it goes!
The daisies chuckle; oh, what a tease,
Nature's little pranks carried by the breeze!

With petals as paper, I write my rhyme,
But the wind steals my notes; oh, what a crime!
They swirl in the air, in a flowery fight,
As I chase after drafts, what a silly sight!

So here in the flowers, laughter remains,
As petals and breezes play fun little games.
With joy wrapped in colors, laughs are the keys,
In this world of blossoms, I dance with the breeze!

Soft Memories in the Garden

In a garden lush and green,
The gnomes dance, quite unseen.
They trip over tulips low,
And giggle as the daisies grow.

A rabbit wore a tiny hat,
While chasing after a sly cat.
Both lost track of time, oh dear!
Who knew they'd both end up here?

Bouncing bumbles sing off-key,
While the sun spills its honey.
Chasing shadows, butterflies,
With laughter echoing through the skies.

So let's frolic, jump and play,
In our silly, garden way.
For every chuckle, every cheer,
Makes these soft memories dear.

Echoes of Rustling Leaves

Leaves are whispering, what a show,
They giggle as they swirl and flow.
Dancing like they own the ground,
With silly sounds that swirl around.

Each step a crunch beneath my feet,
As squirrels dart in their wild retreat.
They pause, then scold with tiny fuss,
While I laugh at their little plus.

The acorns plop like popcorn treats,
Joining in on our fun little beats.
Nature's jesters laugh all day,
As shadows creep and skedaddle away!

So join the dance, let's sway with grace,
As leaves wear smiles upon their face.
In this rustling choir, take a chance,
And join the merry autumn dance.

The Elegance of Withered Foliage

Old leaves strut in their autumn gold,
With stories of the past they've told.
They crinkle up with fashionable flair,
Then tumble down without a care.

An old oak sighs, 'I'm still alive!'
While a maple tries, but won't survive.
They gossip 'bout the weather's tricks,
As winds play tag with their little kicks.

"Look at us!" the dries proclaim,
"Still as quirky as when we came!"
With a twirl here, and a twist there,
They declare victory with much flair.

So raise a glass to leaves all frail,
Who find joy in every trail.
For elegance is often found,
In the rustling laughs that nature's crowned.

Kaleidoscope of Seasonal Journeys

Seasons change with a wink and a grin,
Snowflakes giggle as spring tucks in.
The sun's warm hug gives summer a spin,
While fall whispers, "Let the fun begin!"

In the winter, snowmen wear shades,
While hiding from playful sunrays.
With frosty breath, they dance around,
And stumble as they hit the ground.

Spring awakens in a bright parade,
With flowers swaying, unafraid.
They poke fun at the bees that pry,
With all their buzzing, oh my, oh my!

Summer's heat is a fizzy soda,
Mixing laughter with zesty 'Oh-no's!'
Together we spin through the year,
In a kaleidoscope of joyful cheer.

Soft Prints on the Earth's Canvas

In a garden of giggles, I danced with glee,
A snail outran me, oh how could that be?
The daisies were grinning, the roses turned red,
They laughed at my sneakers, so silly, they said.

With each little footprint, I painted a smile,
Butterflies chuckled, "Stay here for a while!"
The bees buzzed with humor, they tickled my nose,
As I twirled on the grass, wearing sandals and toes.

Finding critters that wore hats and shoes,
A ladybug chef cooking up mushroom stews!
I slipped on some pollen, what a fluffy shock,
The daisies exploded, a tickle party rock!

In this whimsical world where laughter is bright,
I left soft impressions, a giggly delight.
With each jovial step, I added some flair,
Nature's own canvas, painted with care.

Treading through Petal Dust

Stomping through blooms, watch me trip and fall,
I'm the star of the garden, having a ball!
The tulips all snicker as I wipe my chin,
"Next time wear boots!" they giggle, "You win!"

The puddles of nectar beneath my misstep,
Turned my antics to art, what a peculiar prep!
Prancing like a puppy, I launched into space,
With petals as confetti, I danced without grace.

A butterfly guffawed as I splashed in a flower,
Its petals surrendered, oh mighty was my power!
The daisies were rolling in sheer disbelief,
While I fluttered freely, the ultimate thief!

Oh, to tread in this dust where laughter abounds,
With every light step, the humor confounds.
In the chaos of color, the world is so spry,
Treading through petal dust, oh me, oh my!

Whispers in a Floral Maze

In a maze of blooms, I found my way,
Petals held secrets they'd whisper and sway.
"Turn left at the lilac, then right past the bee,"
I giggled and tripped—what a sight to see!

A daffodil chortled, "You've got no sense,
But keep wandering here; it's not too immense!"
The roses winked slyly, they plotted my roam,
As I zigzagged through fancies, I felt quite at home.

Those sneaky old stems showed me the fun,
They twirled and they twinkled, oh how they would run!
I chased after lavender, with mischief in tow,
The petals all howled, in this botanical show.

Whispers of laughter, whirling in glee,
Each flower had its tales, meant just for me.
Through this floral maze, I danced on my toes,
With each silly turn, a new giggle arose.

The Fragrant Odyssey

On a fragrant adventure, I skipped with delight,
With daisies as guides, leading me right.
A whiff of confusion, what happened, oh dear?
I mistook the potpourri for a dinner cheer!

Oh, the lilacs chortled, in fitful surprise,
"Not for eating, dear friend, just look in our eyes!"
The daffodils snickered, "You're quite the delight,
But a salad of petals? Now that's quite a fright!"

Carrying scents of a playful encore,
I danced past the marigolds, bold to explore.
Each sniff was a chuckle, each step was a song,
As I frolicked through fragrance, all merry and strong.

With blossoms as jesters, my day was a blast,
A fragrant odyssey, my worries surpassed.
And as the sun shone, I found this was true,
Laughter's the bloom that forever breaks through.

Sun-Kissed Trails of Color

In the garden where we play,
Colors clash like night and day.
Bumblebees buzz, with no care,
Dancing 'round just like a fair.

Lemons tangle in a vine,
Sipping sunshine, sipping wine.
Mismatched socks upon the grass,
Fashion statements made with sass.

Ladybugs, they twirl and spin,
Chasing ants, they have their grin.
Giggling blooms, they're in a race,
Nature smiles, what a wild place!

Caterpillars munch and laugh,
Sharing their peculiar craft.
In this chaos, colors blend,
Funny how this day won't end!

The Secret Garden's Footfall

Tiptoe through the leafy maze,
Where the flowers play their games.
Frogs wear ties, they croak a tune,
Inviting clouds to dance at noon.

Worms are plotting with the bees,
Making hats from dandelions, if you please!
Wishes float on puffs of air,
While the sun endorses flair!

Daisies count the passing days,
Laughter echoes in sun's rays.
Sneaky squirrels hide their treats,
Playing tag on tiny feet.

Every step's a playful choice,
Nature sings with joyful voice.
Join the fun, get lost in green,
A secret world, vivid and keen!

Imprints of the Timeless Blossom

Flowers giggle, petals sway,
Telling tales of yesterday.
Butterflies chase, think it's a game,
Even the raindrops feel the same.

In this patch of silly sprites,
Giggles echo, pure delights.
Tulips dance in froggy shoes,
Watching clouds play peek-a-boo.

Dandelions blow whimsical dreams,
While the sunlight sparkles and beams.
Every blossom, a joyful jest,
Nature's laughter, the very best.

Hiding secrets, unfurling truth,
Imprints left from innocent youth.
Here in chaos, joy will bloom,
In this garden, fun makes room!

The Serpent of Nature's Vows

A winding trail of color reigns,
Where the gossip of the flowers trains.
Vows are whispered, kissed by sun,
A snake slithers—oh what fun!

He claims to know each flower's name,
Pretends he's wise, oh what a game!
Chasing shadows with a grin,
He hides, then pops back in.

Rabbits laugh at his sly style,
While swirling daisies wink and smile.
The garden's secret dance unfolds,
With tales of laughter, love retold.

In this place of nature's tease,
Whimsical moments float like breeze.
Join the rumors of the vine,
And share a giggle, truly divine!

Serenade of Flora's Lullaby

In gardens bright where daisies dance,
A bee tried hard to woo a chance.
He buzzed in tune, a clumsy croon,
But tripped on petals, oh what a swoon!

With roses red, he took a dive,
And landed soft, yet still alive!
"Just a bump!" he said with glee,
As tulips giggled, wild and free.

The daffodils wore grins so wide,
As bees took flights on flower rides.
They spun and twirled, a silly sight,
A floral show, pure delight!

Underneath the sunlit glow,
Nature's charm stole the show.
With laughter bright in every sway,
A garden serenade at play!

Wandering Through Fragrant Echoes

A clumsy ant with crumbs to claim,
Would march along, but felt the shame.
He met a bloom quite large and round,
And whispered tales, a treasure found!

"Hey flower friend, do you see me?
I'm on an epic quest, quite free!"
But starry petals, oh, they laughed,
As pollen drizzled, sweetly daft.

A butterfly flew by with flair,
And tickled him without a care.
The ant proclaimed, with eyes so wide,
"Next time, a flower, I will ride!"

In fragrant echoes, all around,
Nature's humor joyfully found.
Adventure calls, come join the fun,
With every laugh beneath the sun!

The Pathway of Nature's Heart

On grassy paths where wild blooms blow,
A squirrel dashed with joyful flow.
He stopped to greet a shy grass sprout,
And spun a yarn that left no doubt!

"Did you hear the joke about the bee?
He thought he was good at jamboree!
But buzzing loudly, he missed his mark,
And got quite stuck in a pastry park!"

Laughter echoed, leaves would sway,
As flowers joined the lively play.
They chuckled soft, their colors bright,
A woodland party in pure delight!

With every step, a joke to share,
Among the blooms, a friendly air.
Together they weave, with glee of art,
On the winding path of nature's heart!

Aromatic Adventures Along the Way

Through fields of green where scents collide,
A raccoon danced, with eyes so wide.
He tumbled into fragrant dew,
And found himself; a sweet debut!

With daisies laughing, he took a spin,
"Who knew adventure could start with gin?"
The daisies giggled, and jiggled too,
As he snorted fog, like a morning brew.

A bumblebee buzzed in for a snack,
While our furry friend shared a laugh attack.
"Let's make a brew, with berries sweet,
Nature's punch, a real retreat!"

The laughter soared, the petals twirled,
In every heart, a song unfurled.
As fragrant tales filled the air,
The world giggled, debonair!

Wanderlust in Bloom

In gardens bright, I skipped with glee,
Chasing flowers, oh so free.
A bee chased me, what a flurry!
I ran in circles, oh what a hurry!

Pansies giggled in the sun,
Petunias laughed, oh what fun!
The daisies joined, a joyful crew,
Silly me, I tripped and flew!

The tulips danced with a sway,
They teased me all throughout the day.
I bowed and curtsied, so polite,
But slipped on mud, what a sight!

In every bloom, a joke was found,
With every steps, I twirled around.
A silly day in nature's hall,
With laughter echoing, I recall!

A Tapestry of Nature's Footsteps

I wandered through a vibrant maze,
Where flowers chuckled in a haze.
The lilacs whispered silly things,
As butterflies wore funny rings.

A daffodil with a goofy grin,
Said, "Join the fun, let laughter begin!"
I stumbled on a bumblebee,
It buzzed, "Hey friend, let's have a spree!"

Sunflowers winked, long and tall,
Inviting all to join the ball.
We danced beneath the laughing skies,
While petals fell like silly pies!

Laughter echoes, it fills the air,
With nature's jokes, we have no care.
Each trail I walked, a giggle found,
In the tapestry of laughter bound!

Where Bloom and Soil Embrace

In a patch of dirt, a flower sneezed,
Excusing itself, it looked quite pleased.
A tulip laughed, it didn't hide,
"Bless you, friend! Let's take a ride!"

The daisies joked about my shoes,
"Look at them! They've really lost their hues!"
I laughed along, what a sight,
Nature's humor, pure delight!

In the fields where blooms collide,
The sunbeams shimmer and gently glide.
Every bloom sports a funny hat,
An artful touch, imagine that!

As roots and blooms join hand in hand,
I chuckled with the daisies so grand.
In soil we found such joyful grace,
With nature's jokes, a bright embrace!

A Walk through Floral Memories

I strolled through fields of vibrant hue,
Where blossoms shimmered in morning dew.
A lily winked, it took a bow,
"Hey there buddy, want some chow?"

Roses giggled, twirled in flair,
"Twirling's fun, but watch your hair!"
I spun around, oh what a sight,
Tripped on clovers, lost my flight!

"Remember me?" a peony said,
"We danced last spring, now look ahead!"
Each bloom shared its sweetest tale,
As butterflies rode, they danced like a gale!

With laughter ringing, I wore a grin,
In every petal lies the fun within.
These floral memories, bright and spry,
Lift my heart to the sunny sky!

A Symphony of Colorful Echoes

In the garden where daisies dance,
Butterflies chase a bumblebee's prance.
The tulips sing, a jolly tune,
While a snail takes a selfie in the afternoon.

Laughter bounces on vibrant petals,
A ladybug plays leapfrog with the nettles.
Pansies in purple giggle and sway,
As grasshoppers hop in a goofy ballet.

In hues of yellow, orange, and green,
The flowers scheme for a curious scene.
Meanwhile, a caterpillar makes a witty remark,
Laughing as he rides on a daisy's arc.

So come join the party where colors collide,
In this garden of laughter, take a joyful ride.
With each bloom a chuckle, each leaf a grin,
This symphony of colors, let the fun begin!

Secrets in the Garden's Wake

Underneath the leafy cloak they play,
Dandelions whisper secrets all day.
Rabbits gossip, sharing a tale,
While a sleeping hedgehog dreams without fail.

There's mischief at hand with a wily sweet pea,
Telling jokes to the bees on an enchanted spree.
A mole with a monocle plots with delight,
As fireflies blink in the soft twilight.

The roses chuckle, they have quite the gossip,
While the marigolds dress like a circus; what a trip!
An old gnarled tree grumbles with grace,
Watching the chaos in this wild space.

So listen in close to the whispers of green,
For secrets unfold where laughter is seen.
In this garden, hilarity grows anew,
Where the blooms spill stories, just for you!

Gentle Breezes and Soft Hues

A gentle breeze tickles the blooms,
As daisies dance in their colorful costumes.
With a chuckle or two, they swish and sway,
While the lilacs tell tales of a sunny day.

Buttercups blush in the warm, soft glow,
As petunias strut their stuff in a row.
A squirrel with a hat juggles acorns with flair,
Causing fits of giggles in midair.

The violets are snickering, playing it cool,
While some sunflowers watch as a makeshift school.
The daisies snicker at a gopher's slip,
And the garden bursts out with a joyful trip.

In this whimsical world of laughter and cheer,
Each breeze carries joy that's perfectly clear.
With hues that sing and chuckles that rise,
Welcome to the garden where humor flies!

The Carpet of Daisy Dreams

A carpet laid out, a floral delight,
Where dreams are woven, oh what a sight!
Bouncing on daisies, a frog sings a tune,
With a hat made of clovers, he thinks he's a boon.

The dandelion's laughter floats on a breeze,
While a ladybug rolls with spectacular ease.
Tulips giggle, their colors ablaze,
As they share silly jokes in the sun's warm rays.

In this patch of dreams where the giggles reside,
Worms dance the cha-cha with nothing to hide.
The sunflowers twirl, so tall and so proud,
As a playful wind carries their joyous crowd.

So skip through the blooms, to laughter's sweet song,
Where daisies chuckle and everyone belongs.
In this carpet of dreams, let your spirit take flight,
Join the revelry, oh what a sight!

Harmony in Nature's Embrace

In the garden, bees buzz loud,
A butterfly wearing a flower crown.
The daisies dance, the wind's a clown,
While ants march like a tiny crowd.

Squirrels play tag, oh what a sight,
Chasing shadows, causing a fuss.
The blossoms giggle, without a fright,
As petals fall like confetti in a rush.

A Wandering Heart Among Flowers

Strolling through blooms of every hue,
A bumblebee steals my ice cream.
With sticky fingers and a laugh or two,
Nature's whim feels like a dream.

Tulips wave as I trip and stumble,
Laughter echoes through the glade.
Sunflowers grin, while I fumble,
In this comedic charade.

Reverberations of Wildflower Whispers

Wildflowers gossip, plotting a game,
Their petals tickle the beams of sun.
Each breeze brings forth a namesake fame,
As dandelions see who can run.

With giggles and sprinkles, they sway in tune,
A madcap waltz beneath the trees.
The clouds join in, a fluffy costume,
While grass musters laughter with ease.

Embracing the Sunlit Path

On the sunlit path, I skip and hop,
Surrounded by a riot of colors bright.
A rabbit laughs, won't ever stop,
As daisies sway with pure delight.

Lemons roll by, giggling so loud,
Rolling away with a zesty grin.
The sun high up, say it's allowed,
To chase your joy as the day begins.

Enigma of Blossom-Kissed Roads

On a path of blooms so bright,
Bugs are buzzing in delight.
Every flower plays a prank,
With its colors, oh so dank!

Beehives whisper, 'What a joke!'
As squirrels break the silent yoke.
A butterfly with silly grace,
Chasing shadows, what a race!

Petals fall like careless snow,
Frogs leap high, putting on a show.
Their ribbits mix with flowers' laughter,
In a comedy, we're the masters!

Blossoms wink, they know the score,
Nature laughs from every pore.
Join the fun, don't be a bore,
On this road, there's always more!

In the Company of Spring Fragrance

In spring's fresh breath, we laugh and sway,
Fragrance tickles, come what may.
The daisies giggle, can you hear?
They whisper secrets, oh so clear!

A bumblebee trips on a daffodil,
Spilling nectar, what a thrill!
Dandelions, with their fluffy heads,
Make wishes come true, or so it's said!

A ladybug rolls, oh what a fuss,
Dancing circles, making a fuss.
Where do you think those ants are bound?
To the largest picnic in the ground!

Together we celebrate the humorous bloom,
In gardens rich with nature's perfume.
Each scent is laughter, every sigh delight,
Spring's jovial company makes everything right!

The Dance of Color in the Wind

Colors whirl in a mad parade,
A flower's dance, never delayed.
Sunflowers spin with cheeky grace,
While tulips giggle, take their place!

The breeze brings jokes from beyond the trees,
Telling tales with every tease.
Grasshoppers leap, with a wink and a moan,
As violets chuckle, never alone!

A rainbow sneezes, such a shock!
While petals laugh with every knock.
Who knew nature had such flair?
In color's dance, we lose our care!

Join the party, grab a friend,
And let the bloom-beat never end.
For in this dance, so sweet, so wild,
We find the joy of nature's child!

Traces of Nature's Tenderness

Whisked away on flower's breath,
Nature's giggle, a sweet caress.
Beneath the leaves, a tiny sprite,
Tossing petals, what a sight!

A snail slinks past with witty charm,
Surrounded by blooms, keeping warm.
While ants march to a silly tune,
Chasing shadows beneath a moon!

Laughter echoes through the trees,
As blossoms beam in playful ease.
A robin sings to all who pass,
Each note a wink, like nature's glass!

Within this warmth, we find our bliss,
In every flower, a love-filled kiss.
So let's dance on this gentle ground,
Where traces of joy in blooms abound!

Vanishing Shadows of Petals

In a garden where nothing is still,
A snail races fast, to steal my thrill.
He slides and he glides, with slippery grace,
While I just trip over, turning red in the face.

The daisies are laughing, waving their heads,
As I trip on the thorns, and fall on my spreads.
They summon the bees to join in the fun,
Buzzing around like they've just won a run.

A squirrel's got style, he jumps with a flair,
Flaunting his acorn like he doesn't care.
I try to impress, with a little dance spin,
But the rooster crows loud, and my pride wears thin.

And just when I thought that no one could see,
A flower in pink starts giggling at me.
With laughter so bright, I can't help but smile,
In a garden parade, it's all worth the while.

Trails of Nature's Ink

With a broom made of twigs, I sweep up the leaves,
While a swan on a pond just seems to tease.
He quacks like he's winning a game of charades,
As I dance in the mud, and trip on my blades.

The bees write their stories, buzzing with cheer,
While I try to catch them, end up in the rear.
A daffodil winks, saying, 'Why so sad?'
I shout, 'Not my fault! It's the bugs that I've had!'

Nature's a pen, and I'm ink on the ground,
Spilling my giggles, all twisted around.
With flowers in bloom, and laughter in air,
Who knew muddy boots could lead to such dare?

As shadows stretch far, they paint tales of glee,
While frogs sing their songs, just mocking poor me.
But joy fills the garden, and nothing can fake,
A canvas of chuckles is mine for the take.

Blooms Beneath Our Feet

Stepping on daisies feels like a crime,
But the flowers just giggle, they know it's prime time.
They bloom and they sway, with each little crack,
While I dance on the path, trying not to slack.

A wobbly bee with a lopsided buzz,
Dances around like it's caught in a fuzz.
I join in the fun, doing the worm on the grass,
While the tulips just chuckle, as they watch my mass.

Butterflies flutter like they're stealing the show,
As I trip and I tumble, but still put on a glow.
A dainty little pansy shouts, "Do it again!"
With petals a-blushing, I just can't pretend.

The grass joins the laughter, a tickle my feet,
As I bow to the blossoms, not ready to meet.
The blooms all around, like a jovial fleet,
Every step is a giggle, life feels so sweet.

Circles of Colorful Whispers

In a circle of daisies, secrets unfold,
With giggles and whispers, they're braver than bold.
They tease at the breeze, while I hop in delight,
Chasing my thoughts like a shadow at night.

The tulips take turns sharing tales of the sun,
While I stumble around, pretending I'm fun.
A butterfly flutters, taking notes with a grin,
Daring me next, to leap, flop, or spin.

Even the grass wants to join in the play,
Tickling my ankles, it won't let me stray.
With colors that chatter, they spark my own laugh,
In circles of whimsy, we dance on this path.

So here in this circle, where life's silliness twirls,
With nature's own laughter, forget all my swirls.
Each bloom has a story, a chuckle to give,
In circles of colors, we dance and we live.

Blossoms Beneath Our Feet

As we stroll through the park, a sight so bizarre,
Flowers dance in the breeze, a bright little spar.
Trying to tiptoe, but oops, there I go,
Tripping on daisies, stealing the show.

Look at the dandelions, they think they're tough,
Blowing their seeds like they're made of fluff.
Each little puffball a tumbleweed tease,
Rolling away laughing, on a whim with the breeze.

We laugh at the poppies that sway with delight,
In a game of hide and seek in the bright sunlight.
Stepping on violets, I hear them complain,
"Can you watch where you're going, or is it a game?"

So next time you wander where blossoms do bloom,
Mind your step, or you'll invoke nature's gloom.
With giggles and chuckles, beneath the blue skies,
Every step's a fun stumble, a sweet surprise.

Aroma of the Winding Way

On the path filled with scents, what do we find?
Fragrant surprises, oh, nature's unkind!
Munching on petals, I made a big mess,
Now I smell like a salad, oh what a dress!

Jasmine whispers sweetly, "Come take a sniff!"
While clovers and grass play a mischievous riff.
Forget not the lilies, so prim and so proper,
But shuffle through daisies? You'll be a flower hopper!

Meet my friend the bee, buzzing round with pride,
Mocking my strut as I swiftly slide.
We giggle together at the folly so fine,
Who knew the great outdoors could taste like a brine?

With each new aroma, I trip and I sway,
These whiffs of bouquet lead me astray.
But laughing out loud, I'll take all the blame,
In a fragrant adventure, it's all just a game!

Nature's Colorful Carpet

Here I go, stepping on bundles of joy,
A lively patch where flowers annoy.
With colors so vivid, a vibrant display,
I'm now part of nature's jazzy ballet!

The roses are giggling, the tulips stand proud,
While I do the cha-cha beneath the crowd.
Falling on pansies, oh what a sight,
Spreading out broader, then laughing with fright.

With each little glide, I'm outright amazed,
Nature's a canvas with colors ablaze.
Forget about dancing, I'm tripping instead,
Rolling through daisies with joy in my head!

So come join the merriment, skip without care,
Twirling through petals, it's quite the affair.
In this colorful carpet, let's tumble and leap,
In nature's embrace, our joy runs deep!

Tracks of Delicate Dreams

Each step we take leaves a mark in the soil,
Twirling and whirling, we're bound to uncoil.
Lost in the laughter of flowers we find,
A trail of giggles that's uniquely designed.

Sunflowers watch with a grin from their place,
As we try out our moves without any grace.
Our shadows do tango, how silly we seem,
Painting the landscape with tracks of our dream.

Oh, look at that butterfly, flapping with flair,
"Do keep up, dear humans, you know I'm not rare!"
Chasing our thoughts, as we tumble and spin,
In this waltz of nature, how did we begin?

So let's leave our marks, every step a delight,
Creating a story in morning's soft light.
With laughter as the soundtrack, we frolic with glee,
In these delicate dreams, just you and me.

www.ingramcontent.com/pod-product-compliance
Lightning Source LLC
Chambersburg PA
CBHW071818160426
43209CB00003B/132